STUDLEY
THROUGH TIME

The rare 'Penfold' pillar box, made in 1866 by Grove and Cochrane of Dudley, that was sited on the western verge of the Alcester Road opposite its junction with Spernal Lane. The box was moved 180 yards north within the village at a later date, where it was unfortunately destroyed following a vehicle accident in 2001. *Courtesy Raymond Lamb.*

STUDLEY
THROUGH TIME

Edited by Alistair Brewin

BREWIN BOOKS

BREWIN BOOKS
19 Enfield Ind. Estate,
Redditch,
Worcestershire,
B97 6BY

www.brewinbooks.com

First published by Brewin Books 2016

Reprinted December 2018
Reprinted April 2021
Reprinted April 2022

© Alistair Brewin 2016

A CIP catalogue record for this book is
available from the British Library.

ISBN: 978-1-85858-555-0

Printed and bound in Great Britain
by Halstan & Co. Ltd.

CONTENTS

Priory Square, 2016, showing Studley's tribute to its needle industry. Installed on September 9th, 2011 the artwork depicts many aspects of village life. In an interview with the Redditch Standard artist Julie Ward explained that: "Nature was a big theme. The River Arrow is represented with an arrow, the fish found there, and wildlife and flowers found at the water's edge. The elephant was the logo that appeared on packets of Studley Needles, and the fish hook reminds us that these were also made here. The gold thread forming the name Studley links to its Anglo Saxon origins – Stud meaning horse, and Ley meaning open field. The horse also reflects the name and the beer mug and barley sheaf were inspired by the local publican trade. The final symbol is of the historically important parish church." *Editor's collection.*

INTRODUCTION

Having lived in Studley for nearly 40 years, I have witnessed many changes within the village, some major others less so. When attempting to dig up more information, I realised just how few books had been published on the village's history, which is when this project began. Rather than attempting to record a comprehensive history of the village or reproducing a photograph of every prominent place and person, I have, in effect, attempted to create a pictorial scrapbook from the resources available. Hopefully some of these images will help to conjure up a flavour of the past from the olden days to much more recent times. A bit of good old fashioned nostalgia if you will.

Apologies if I have inadvertently failed to credit an image. Several of the photos included here have trickled through various people's hands before reaching these pages. Unfortunately some of these treasured images do not have exact details of when they were taken or by whom. Please feel free to email me with further details, should you have them, and I will be delighted to include them in a future edition.

If you have any interesting images of the village that you are willing to share, please email details to the address below or write in to the address on page four. I'm sure there is more than enough material out there for a companion volume!

I would like to take this opportunity to thank all the contributors. In particular I would like to acknowledge John Shakles and Karen Cording from Studley Local History Group (SLHG) for supplying several of the images published here. John and Karen work tirelessly on 'The Studley Historian' magazine which I would wholeheartedly recommend to anyone with an interest in the village. I would also like to thank Judy Ash for letting me use some of the photographs which have previously featured in her excellent calendars of the village. Thanks also to Penny Turner for scouring the RLSS archives in order to find images of the Queen Mother's visit. Finally, I would like to thank Ray Lamb for his invaluable input into the project.

Alistair Brewin
admin@brewinbooks.com

Right: The editor at the front of
Studley Carnival Procession, Crooks Lane, c.1983.

Priory Square and The Barley Mow, c.1900. The pub originally had a brewery at the far end backing onto the Alcester Road, this was subsequently demolished. *Editor's collection.*

Bulldozers clearing snow during the harsh winter of 1947. *Courtesy SLHG.*

An advertisement card for The Barley Mow, c.1921. The building is the village's oldest pub, an internal timber has been found at the property inscribed with a date of 1534. *Courtesy SLHG.*

A more recent shot taken in 2006. The building remains the most photogenic of all Studley's pubs. Note that Studley Self Serve petrol station is visible in the background prior to demolition. *Courtesy Judy Ash.*

Above: Alcester Road in 1906 complete with Studley's most recently lost pub, The Duke of Marlborough, on the far right. *Editor's collection.*

Below: Built c.1725, it is probable that the pub was designed by Francis Smith who was also responsible for Studley Manor House. Seen here in the 1990s the pub had changed little in its outwards appearance. *Courtesy SLHG.*

Above: To the left is The Duke of Marlborough with Centre Service Station on the right, c.1980s. Note the petrol prices. *Courtesy Arthur Daniels.*

Below right: Here's the same shot today. Ironically where the lively Duke of Marlborough once stood now stands a retirement complex. Meanwhile flats now occupy the land where the petrol station and garage were situated. *Editor's collection.*

Above: The Duke of Marlborough sign which stood proudly outside the pub for many years. Reputedly a resident still has the sign safely tucked away in their shed! *Courtesy Arthur Daniels.*

Above: The Bell Brewery and Pub, Alcester Road, in July 1929 ready for the visit of The Duchess of York to Studley Castle. Originally the premises was both a brewery and a public house. Thompson's Bell Brewery was established in 1882 and lasted until 1960 when the business was acquired by Mitchells and Butlers. The last beer was brewed on site during the 1960s. The site where the brewery once stood is now occupied by the beer garden. *Editor's collection.*

Right: Thompson's Milk Stout bottle label. *Editor's collection.*

Below: The Bell in more recent times before its 2015 refurbishment. *Courtesy Judy Ash.*

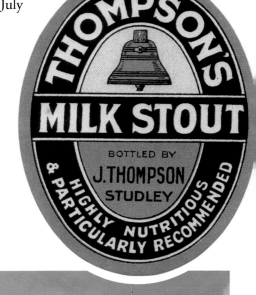

John Thompson brewer advertisement taken from a 1900 Redditch directory. *Courtesy SLHG.*

Above left: Formerly The Nags Head, the Redditch Road pub was renamed The Victoria Works in 2012 after the disused needle works opposite. The pub is the Weatheroak Brewery Tap House selling beer brewed at their micro brewery on the opposite side of the road at the Royal Victoria Works. Beers include: Victoria Works, Light Oak and St. Udley Mild. *Editor's collection.*

Above right: The Nags Head taken in 1931, the landlord Alfred Pinfield stands nonchalantly outside his establishment. *Courtesy SLHG.*

Right: Weatheroak Brewery pump graphic. *Editor's collection.*

Below: The Nags Head taken in 2006. Before the national relaxation in licensing The Nags Head was the first pub in the village to have a late licence. *Courtesy Judy Ash.*

Above: The original Jubilee Inn was located on Littlewood Green close to the existing pub. Seen here c.1910 it is now a house. *Courtesy Raymond Lamb.*

Right: The 'new' Jubilee Inn, built 1938, on a cold winter's morning 2010. The pub had briefly been closed but reopened on 27th November. *Editor's collection.*

1953 Coronation Party outside the current Jubilee Inn, Bromsgrove Road. *Courtesy SLHG.*

The Bricklayers Arms on the corner of Toms Town and Alcester Road, c.1900.
Courtesy Bill McCarthy.

Left: The Bricklayers Arms was purchased in 1989 by Colm O'Rourke's pub chain and renamed The Little Lark. The decor was based around a fictitious newspaper publication entitled 'The Little Lark' complete with printing press. *Courtesy John Shakles.*

Below: In 2007 the pub simply became known as The Lark. It has since been taken over and, once again, is now called The Little Lark. The press has now been moved indoors. *Courtesy Judy Ash.*

Studley Fire Brigade outside The Swan Inn, High Street, c.1890. The licensee was Alfred Richards. *Courtesy Geoff Vale.*

Above: The Swan Inn in 1997. The Italian restaurant next door was still open. *Courtesy John Shakles.*

Left: The Swan Inn in 1976. The Italian restaurant next door was yet to be built. *Editor's collection.*

Above: The Griffin pub in Green Lane originally formed part of a larger needle manufactory called the Towers. During the late 1800s the pub was referred to as both The Needlemakers Arms and The Griffin. *Courtesy Raymond Lamb.*

Left: Token for The Needlemakers Arms pub which later became known as The Griffin. Not to be confused with the pub of the same name in Watts Road! *Courtesy SLHG.*

Below: Whilst the factory was demolished, for many years, the pub remained intact. During the 1980s the site was subject to a compulsory purchase order to make way for a bypass that was never built. The pub subsequently reopened and is seen here c.1990 but later closed for good. Sadly, The Griffin has now fallen into disrepair and is due for demolition. *Courtesy John Shakles.*

Two more of Studley's lost pubs.

Above: The Coach and Horses, c.1905. The pub was later known as The Central Restaurant Public House. The building is now a shop and is located on the High Street behind Studley Fish Bar. *Courtesy Raymond Lamb.*

Below: The Grove Inn, Crooks Lane, c.1920. The licensee was James E. Huband, seen here seated, middle row, centre shot. The pub was previously known as The Hog In The Hole. The property was demolished c.1960. *Courtesy SLHG.*

The Needlemakers Arms, Watts Road, c.1930, prior to an extension during the 1950s. Pictured here is a member of the Huband family. The landlord James E. Huband had moved here from The Grove Inn. The history of Studley's pubs, before 1940, is covered in Richard Churchley's booklet 'Having a drink round Studley'. *Courtesy Raymond Lamb.*

The Royal Oak, Alcester Road, 2007.
Previously known as The Brewers Arms.
Courtesy Judy Ash.

The Railway Inn, Station Road, c.1995.
Previously known as The Railway Tavern.
Courtesy John Shakles.

Right: Studley's annual wheelbarrow race, 2013. The event was established in 1975 and is held in aid of good causes. The rules are simple; take it in turns to push or be pushed around each village pub in a wheelbarrow, having a pint at every stop!
Courtesy Emma Smith.

Left: Stud Bitter beer mat. The Washford Mill is purported to be Studley's oldest needle factory. In 1978 Mill based Studley Brewery brewed its own beer, including Stud Bitter, Old Glory and Studley Giant, up until its closure in 1982. *Editor's collection.*

The Needlemakers Arms, Watts Road, 2007. *Courtesy Judy Ash.*

The Shakespeare Inn, Redditch Road, 1997.
Courtesy John Shakles.

Studley Old Police Station c.1960, built 1894. The replacement police station was built next door on Bell Lane but has now been demolished. Today the left side is a house whilst the right side has been turned into residential and office accommodation. *Courtesy SLHG.*

In the mid 1960s Boots The Chemist built new premises on the corner of the Alcester Road and Bell Lane. During the 1980s the building became Ampower video shop, renting and selling video tapes and computer games. It is now home to AK Fitted Interiors Limited. *Courtesy Raymond Lamb.*

During the 1980s the right hand side of the Old Police Station sold and repaired lawnmowers. *Courtesy John Shakles.*

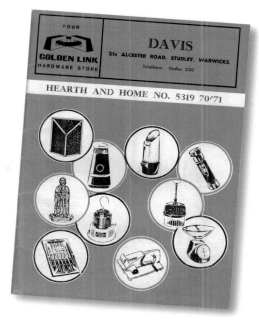

A 1970/71 Davis' product catalogue. *Courtesy SLHG.*

A little further up the Alcester Road is one of Studley's most well known and well loved shops; Davis' hardware store. The editor remembers spending many a Saturday afternoon rifling through endless 5p and 10p toy jars. Davis' still retains its iconic sign which is now well over 50 years old. *Courtesy Judy Ash.*

Above: An early shot of the Alcester Road taken c.1930. *Courtesy SLHG.*

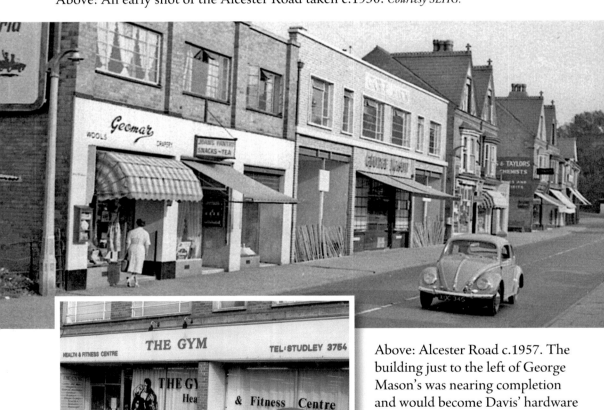

Above: Alcester Road c.1957. The building just to the left of George Mason's was nearing completion and would become Davis' hardware store. *Courtesy Phillip Wainwright.*

Left: Studley Gym took over George Mason's old premises until its closure in 2006. *Editor's collection.*

Above: Alcester Road c.1957 taken from the bottom of Marble Alley. Huins' shoe shop used an early pedoscope machine which took X-ray pictures of customers' feet. Lloyds Bank's premises would eventually be built in the space next door to Timothy Whites' shop. *Courtesy Phillip Wainwright.*

Left: A similar view today. *Editor's collection.*

Left: Alcester Road 1997 with lollipop lady Sheila Robeson on duty. Johnson's has changed to Studley News and Dillons has replaced the Kwik Save supermarket.
Courtesy John Shakles.

Above: Alcester Road c.1960. For many years Johnson's traded as a popular Post Office, sweetshop and newsagents. *Editor's collection.*

Left: H Johnson Post Office 1d token. *Courtesy SLHG.*

The Grange, Alcester Road, c.1910. The gardens to the rear were sold off to become a carpark for the supermarket which was built next door. The building to the left was called Bank House and comprised of a grocery shop, belonging to Robert Oakley, called Bank House Stores and The Metropolitan Bank. *Courtesy Raymond Lamb.*

Alcester Road as it is today. Studley News has now become a restaurant and Bank House has been demolished to make way for a Supermarket. The Grange now has less ornate bay windows and has become an office block. *Editor's collection.*

Further down the Alcester Road c.1900 taken by C E Griffiths. To the right behind gates, is Albion House, listed grade II, with its needle manufactory just out of shot. Hidden behind trees, centre shot, is the former Doctor's Surgery which is now PSW Art Supplies. *Courtesy SLHG.*

A similar view from the opposite direction c.1960s, looking towards The Duke of Marlborough. Note the large Guinness advert. The black and white cottage to the far right was originally a police station and is listed grade II. *Courtesy SLHG.*

The Alcester Road, Squire's Hill, 1903. *Courtesy SLHG.*

Taken in the early 1980s, the general stores can still be seen to the left. When the stores closed, the shop front was removed and it was used as a base for a local taxi firm before becoming residential accommodation. Further down the old Co-operative building can be seen now complete with its prominent clock. *Courtesy SLHG.*

Alcester Co-operative Society's Grocery and Drapery, Studley, 1910. *Courtesy SLHG.*

The same street scene in 2013. The clock no longer hangs outside the old Co-operative building, which is now a wedding shop. To the far left is a small housing development where the Manse was originally situated. *Editor's collection.*

Once quite a substantial building, the Manse on Alcester Road was left to fall apart. The site was eventually redeveloped with modern terraced housing. *Courtesy SLHG.*

Above: The Manse prior to demolition. *Courtesy John Shakles.*

Right: The Manse site as it looks today. *Editor's collection.*

Opposite the Manse lies Studley Manor House which was originally known as New Hall. Designed by Francis Smith it is seen here in 1910. Built c.1725 for the Chambers family it is thought that this building was, at one time, the residence of the Knottesford family recalled today in the street name Knottesford Close. The property is listed grade II*. *Editor's collection.*

On 25th June 1981 the Queen Mother visited Studley Manor House to open the new Royal Life Saving Society's headquarters which were to be located there. The new base was to be called Mountbatten House in honour of Lord Mountbatten. *Courtesy RLSS.*

Above: Some of the 600 guests leaving Gillett Court, Mountbatten House after the Opening Ceremony and Garden Party. *Courtesy RLSS.*

Above: Beneath Her Personal Standard, The Queen Mother with Prince Michael and senior Society Officers watches Countess Mountbatten of Burma plant an oak tree to commemorate her Father's association with the Society. *Courtesy RLSS.*

Right: The Queen Mother meets Mountbatten staff. *Courtesy RLSS.*

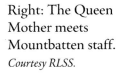

Above: A panoramic view of the Society's Commonwealth Headquarters from the south west, with the new Hong Kong Room (designed by Michael Jackson Associates) and the swimming pool in Ward Court. *Courtesy RLSS.*

"I am so delighted to be in Studley once again, for I remember so well my visit to this beautiful countryside a long time ago in 1929.

It is now 20 years since I opened the first Commonwealth Conference in London and today marks the end of your Fifth Conference. During this time a great deal has happened to reduce the number of deaths by drowning. Education by the family and in schools, using new equipment and imaginative methods, has stimulated interest and last year nearly one million people throughout the Commonwealth qualified as lifesavers. Nevertheless, there can be no room for complacency and I am therefore very pleased to learn that the future development of life saving, with particular emphasis on extending the influence of the Society in other countries, has been the keynote of this year's conference.

Lord Mountbatten became the President of the Society at the request of the King in 1945. His personal initiative on his visits abroad continued the expansion of the numbers in Branches in Commonwealth countries and then the granting of the Supplemental Royal Charter in 1960 established the new Commonwealth Council. The emergence of the first National Branches was due to his wisdom and guidance.

This new Headquarters will be a lasting memorial to Lord Mountbatten whose vision and leadership in times of war and peace have made him a legend not only in our Country but in all nations throughout the world.

And now it gives me great pleasure to unveil the plaque and portrait and declare open Mountbatten House."

Above: The Queen Mother's speech. She had been to the village previously in 1929 to visit Studley Castle. *Courtesy RLSS.*

Right: The plaque that still remains outside the house which, today, is in private hands. *Editor's collection.*

MOUNTBATTEN HOUSE
COMMONWEALTH HEADQUARTERS
OF
THE ROYAL LIFE SAVING SOCIETY
1980

Before B&Q's stranglehold of the DIY market Tony's Handyman Centre, High Street, was the place to go. Seen here in 1997 at the rear wood was cut to customers exact dimensions. Part of the building was eventually demolished to make way for access to a small new housing development at the rear. *Courtesy John Shakles.*

Alcester Co-operative Society's butchers shop window, High Street, Studley, 1957. *Courtesy SLHG.*

Looking up Fleece Hill, High Street c.1957 with The Swan Inn on the horizon.
Courtesy Phillip Wainwright.

An earlier view of Station Road with The Swan Inn in the background. Note the horse drawn cart. The building to the far right is the Schoolmaster's House built in 1857. Next door is the National School which was built in 1850. *Courtesy SLHG.*

Above: Station Road c.1930s. All the buildings to the left still survive to this day. Note the absence of Eldorado Close as the estate behind it was yet to be built. *Editor's collection.*

Below: A wonderful shot of B&L Bott grocers and confectioners of Station Road c.1960. The building became a butchers and is now an office. *Courtesy SLHG.*

THE COMMON, STUDLEY.

Above: The top of Station Road was once known as The Common, the area stretched until the Railway Inn. Fields and farms, on both sides of the street, separated it from lower down Station Road. *Courtesy SLHG.*

Below: A later 1950s photo of the same view. One of the houses has now become a general store. *Courtesy Phillip Wainwright.*

Marble Alley (left) has changed much over the years. Above c.1900. *Editor's collection.*

Corner of Marble Alley and High Street 1997. *Courtesy John Shakles.*

Looking up Marble Alley with Lisa's cafe on the right, 1997. *Courtesy John Shakles.*

Marble Alley during 1997.
Courtesy John Shakles.

Marble Alley's popular McKee's restaurant in 2006. *Courtesy Judy Ash.*

Above left: Marble Alley, 1911, looking towards High Street. The road was formerly known as Marble Terrace. *Courtesy SLHG.*

Above right: 1990s advertisement for Marble Alley store 'Interesting Things'. *Editor's collection.*

Recent times have seen the conversion of all of the shops and the restaurant into housing. The buildings to the left are the rear of the new Co-operative supermarket. *Editor's collection.*

Above: Foster's Stores, Redditch Road, taken around 1920. Note the garage to the left of the main stores. *Courtesy SLHG.*

Below: The property is currently the home of Planscapes and The Heat Store. *Editor's collection.*

Above: Looking up Redditch Road c.1904, with The Nag's Head in the distance. Foster's is on the right. *Courtesy Arthur Daniels.*

Inset below: In the 70s, 80s and 90s the property became an off licence called Bob's Wines. *Editor's collection.*

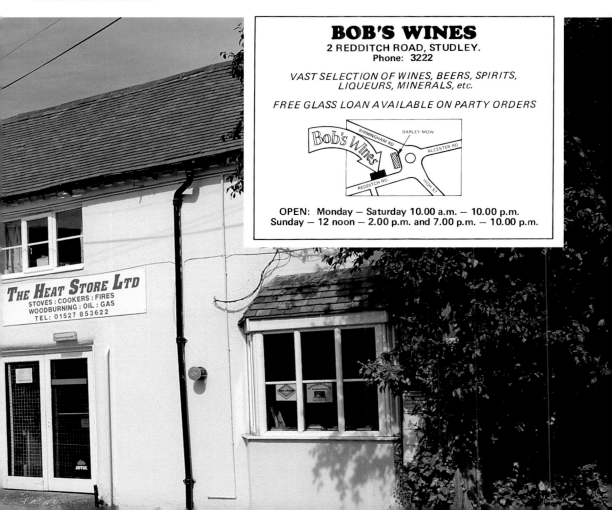

BOB'S WINES
2 REDDITCH ROAD, STUDLEY.
Phone: 3222

VAST SELECTION OF WINES, BEERS, SPIRITS, LIQUEURS, MINERALS, etc.

FREE GLASS LOAN AVAILABLE ON PARTY ORDERS

OPEN: Monday — Saturday 10.00 a.m. — 10.00 p.m.
Sunday — 12 noon — 2.00 p.m. and 7.00 p.m. — 10.00 p.m.

THE HEAT STORE LTD
STOVES : COOKERS : FIRES
WOODBURNING : OIL : GAS
TEL: 01527 853622

Above: The Wapping, Redditch Road c.1950. The large house to the far right was called The Laurels. All the houses were later demolished. *Courtesy Brett Coldicott.*

Left: Rear view of the Wapping from Recreation Ground. *Courtesy Brett Coldicott.*

Below: A further view of the Wapping, Redditch Road. Retirement bungalows have replaced these buildings. *Courtesy Brett Coldicott.*

Above: The Convent, New Road, Studley c.1910. Part of the Catholic school can be seen to the left of the house, on the corner of New Road and Church Street (just out of shot). *Courtesy SLHG.*

Right: New Road in 1997. The Catholic school and convent had both become AD Assemblies' factory. *Courtesy John Shakles.*

Below right: New Road today. The convent and school were demolished to make way for new housing. *Editor's collection.*

Below: Laying of sewers, New Road, Studley c.1923. *Courtesy Bill McCarthy.*

A shop that many residents have a soft spot for is R.W. Rutter's store, on the corner of Bromsgrove Road and Littlewood Green. Pictured here in 2006, R.W. Rutter has been trading from these premises since 1952. The single storey section of the building was once a blacksmith's workshop. *Courtesy Judy Ash.*

The top of Node Hill, Bromsgrove Road, complete with Flowers Beer lorry, c.1950. *Courtesy SLHG.*

Right: A brick manufactured by Victoria Brickworks, Studley. Brickmaking is still remembered in the street name Brickyard Lane. *Courtesy SLHG.*

Below: Studley brickworks prior to demolition in the 1960s. *Courtesy SLHG.*

Bottom. Studley brickworks in action c.1930. *Courtesy SLHG.*

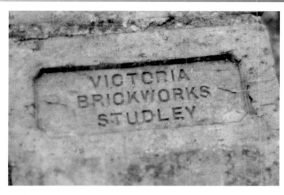

Above: VE Day Party in Watts Road, May 1945. *Courtesy Miriam Watkins (née Sutor).*

Left: New council houses in Watts Road, formerly known as Watts Lane, not long after completion, c.1924. *Courtesy Bill McCarthy.*

Below: Foster's van doing the rounds in Outhill, Studley, c.1920. *Courtesy Harry Taylor.*

Above: Studley discharged and demobilised soldiers and sailors, 1919. *Courtesy Kath Weaver (née Mills).*

Right: Hardings coaches parked in Foster Avenue ready to take Studley holiday makers on a trip to Weston-super-Mare. *Courtesy Sybil Watton.*

Below: 1911 Coronation procession with Studley Fire Brigade passing through. *Courtesy SLHG.*

Left side elevation of The Vicarage in its heyday, c.1930. *Courtesy SLHG.*

Sadly, The Vicarage fell into disrepair and was demolished. The Vicarage Hall to the right was retained and can still be seen today. *Courtesy Arthur Daniels.*

Above: Studley Fete, c.1935. The Vicarage Hall is in the background. The former British Prime Minister Anthony Eden is standing third man from the right. The little girl to the right is Brenda Lancaster (née Hill). *Courtesy SLHG.*

Left: The Foredraught c.1957. The lane was eventually redeveloped and all the buildings shown here were demolished. *Courtesy Phillip Wainwright.*

Above: Catholic church, village procession, Alcester Road, passing Manor Park Road, c.1912.
Editor's collection.

Left: Birmingham Road, c.1920. A modern photo of the houses on the right can be seen on page 87.
Courtesy SLHG.

Below: The River Arrow, 1924 from a photo by C E Griffiths. *Courtesy SLHG.*

Above: Studley Infants School during the Coronation year of 1953. *Courtesy Janet Hollington (née Shrimpton).*

Right: John Foster outside Central Stores, High Street, which is now 45 High Street, c.1900. *Courtesy SLHG.*

Below: 1953 Pram Race at the former POW Camp, Holt Farm. The buildings were used as family homes after 1948. *Courtesy SLHG.*

Above: Top end of Castle Road/Alcester Road showing 'Claremont' after the house had been extended, c.1900. *Courtesy SLHG.*

Left: An earlier shot of 'Claremont' before its extension and with the smithy still intact at the back. The building is now listed grade II*. *Courtesy SLHG.*

Bottom end of Castle Road c.1900. *Courtesy Pat Wharrad.*

Above: VE Day Street Party, 8th May 1945. Looking down Redditch Road towards the village centre. These houses were demolished to make way for Crendon Close. *Courtesy Geoff Vale.*

Left: Foster Avenue street party, c.1950s. *Courtesy SLHG.*

Below: Carnival Float taking part in the 1988 Studley Carnival procession, Alcester Road. *Courtesy Alan Brewin.*

Above: Priory Farm, 1948.
Courtesy SLHG.

Right: Studley in Bloom team taking a well earned break from tending to the village's flowers, 2016.
Courtesy Terry Burton.

Below: Lighting the beacon for the Queen's 90th birthday celebrations, Crooks Lane Recreational Ground, 21st April 2016. *Courtesy Terry Burton.*

Above: Studley Tigers Cycle Speedway team, c.1940. *Courtesy Mary Brazil (née Watton).*

Left: Needle Industries Sporting FC, c.1980. *Courtesy Val Blundell.*

Below: Studley CC, 1955-6. *Courtesy Peter Bolt.*

STUDLEY ROVERS. F.C. 1935-36
WINNERS REDDITCH JUNIOR LEAGUE-R.L.H. CUP.
POLICE "C" & KELLETT CUPS, PHOTO, JOE HARMAN.

Above: Studley Rovers FC, 1935-1936. John Thompson is holding the shield. *Courtesy SLHG.*

Right: Allendale FC, c.1970. *Courtesy Val Blundell.*

Below: Studley Entaco bowling club during the 1960s. *Courtesy SLHG.*

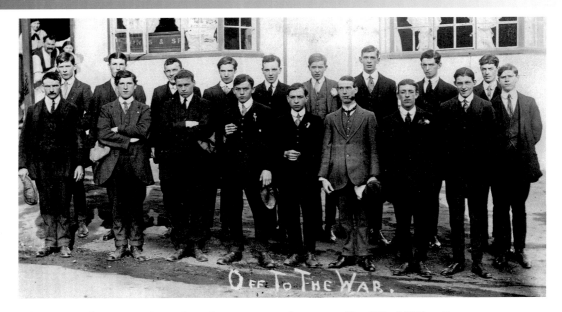

Above: Studley men who enlisted in 1914, ready to go off to World War One.
Courtesy Anne Bradford.

Above: Brave Studley men off to World War One, Priory Square, 1914. *Courtesy Anne Bradford.*

Right: The unveiling of Studley's War Memorial on the Alcester Road c.1921. More information about those inscribed on the memorial can be found in Arthur Cooke's poignant booklet 'In Memory of 100 Studley men who gave their lives in World War One'. *Courtesy SLHG.*

Studley's connection with needle making goes back over 350 years. Many of the smaller needle businesses dotted around the village were subsequently taken over by William Hall. During 1930 the company became known as ENTACO (English Needle and Fishing Tackle Co. Ltd), changing again to Needle Industries in 1946, before being purchased in 1973 by Coats Paton. A detailed account of Studley's needlemaking can be found in Richard Churchley's booklet 'Needlemakers in Alcester, Sambourne and Studley'.

A 1970s photo of Priory Square with Needle Industries' Central Works in the background. The quaint black and white cottage survived demolition and is listed grade II, a current photo is shown on page six. *Courtesy John Shakles.*

Marble Alley, c.1960, showing the rear elevation of Needle Industries' Central Works. *Courtesy Brett Coldicott.*

VJ Day 1945 at the Entaco canteen which was at the bottom of Marble Alley/Alcester Road.
Courtesy SLHG.

Another later photo of the Entaco canteen with The Bell pub just visible in the background.
Courtesy SLHG.

Needle manufacturing at William Hall & Co., 1915. The building stood on Fleece Hill, Bromsgrove Street (now known as High Street), on what is currently part of the derelict Co-operative site. The works eventually became part of Needle Industries. This photograph was taken by Arthur W Utton who was a photographer based at The Studio, Priory Square. Note the First World War recruiting poster on the far right. *Courtesy SLHG.*

Fleece Hill, early 1920s. To the left is Hemmings & Sons Grocers, which is now Ellis Maintenance Services Ltd. In the background is the Barley Mow, to the right is William Hall & Co. which was previously The Golden Fleece Inn. *Courtesy SLHG.*

William Hall & Co. factory burning down c.1977. Local children put their Raleigh Choppers to one side in amazement. *Courtesy Bill McCarthy.*

1940s 'Sphinx Brand' AG Baylis & Sons gramophone needle tin. AG Baylis & Sons was another company that was absorbed into the mighty Needle Industries empire. *Editor's collection.*

A pack of Milward's knitters needles. Note the company's famous iron fist logo. Milward's also became part of Needle Industries. *Courtesy Julie Brewin.*

An Air Raid warning exercise c.1940. Needle industry workers leaving the factory and crossing the Birmingham Road. *Courtesy SLHG.*

A 1930s Entaco works outing. *Courtesy SLHG.*

Needle Industries packaging workshop. Workers are placing needles into packets, the supervisor, Bill Spray, is in the background, May 1969. *Courtesy Bill McCarthy.*

A 1960s photo of Needle Industries' Arrow Works, on the Birmingham Road. *Editor's collection.*

During the 1960s Needle Industries was the largest manufacturer of needles in the world, employing 15,000 people, however by the late 1980s the business had fallen into decline. In 1991 there was a management buyout and the business was renamed Entaco Ltd. Needlemaking continued in the village on a smaller scale until the company moved to Redditch. According to Studley resident Val Blundell, Entaco manager Dave Gibbs produced the very last needle at the Studley site, in the form of a Bodkin Size 17, during September 2007. There are several interesting accounts of needle making in Studley and Redditch in Anne Bradford's fascinating book 'Old Redditch Voices'.

Above: Completed in 1836, Studley Castle has an interesting and varied past. The building was constructed as a mansion for baronet Francis Lyttleton Holyoake Goodricke. Subsequently the property was purchased by Lady Warwick who opened up the Studley Agricultural College for Women in 1903. When the college closed in 1969 the building was taken over by British Leyland, later known as Rover Cars, who used it as a conference venue. In 1979 BL's Heritage Collection archives also moved there. As a young boy the editor remembers having a guided tour and being shown Paddy Hopkirk's Monte Carlo winning Mini. The car collection eventually moved to Gaydon and, with the demise of Rover, the building became a hotel. *Editor's collection.*

Right: Studley Castle Agricultural College for Women, 1910. *Courtesy SLHG.*

Studley Castle Lodges, 1904. *Editor's collection.*

Studley Castle Lodges, 2013. The righthand side has now fallen into disrepair. Both the lodges are listed grade II whilst the Castle itself is listed grade II*. *Editor's collection.*

STUDLEY COLLEGE originated as a hostel, founded at Reading in 1898 by Frances, Lady Warwick, for those desiring to fit themselves for an outdoor life. In 1903 it moved to Warwickshire and became a separate teaching centre for gardening and dairying. Development proceeded steadily, existing departments were enlarged, others added, and the number of students increased. Including those taking short courses, over 1,200 have passed through the College, many of whom are now managing their own land or earning salaries. Many are in the Dominions, and horticulture and agriculture are among the few professions where the demand for women workers exceeds the supply. The College is now recognised by the Ministry of Agriculture and Fisheries and an annual grant of £1,000 has been made by that department towards its maintenance since 1926.

In 1911, Miss L. A Hamilton, M.D., the then Warden, obtained a lease of Studley Castle Estate, having taken over full responsibility when Lady Warwick, in 1909, found it necessary to relinquish the active part she had taken in organising the College. To manage the affairs of the College. Miss Hamilton formed a Company in 1916 under the licence of the Board of Trade, it being made a condition that all income of the College be applied solely towards the objects of the College, and that no profits accrue to the managers. She retired from active work shortly before her death in 1925.

The Lease is now drawing to a close and it is essential to secure the future of the College and to ensure the continuance of its important work by the acquisition of the freehold. The Governors, with the approval of the Ministry of Agriculture, are endeavouring to raise the necessary funds. An option to purchase has been secured and the Treasury has promised a grant, on a pound for pound basis, up to £5,000. The Governors therefore are appealing for donations towards :—

(a) Ten thousand pounds to complete the purchase of Studley Castle and 340 acres of land and to make available the Treasury grant.

(b) A further ten thousand pounds to put into repair and enlarge the farm buildings, improve the milking herd, reorganise the poultry department, provide new laboratories, and fill other definite wants. These include a library, an iris garden, fruit room for storing, range of new plant houses, refrigerating plant, Dutch barn, and milking machine.

Thus a total of £20,000 is needed to enable the College to cope adequately with present requirements and train efficiently the 60 students it accommodates. Should the demand for competent and educated farm, garden and dairy workers continue to increase, further extension will be necessary in the immediate future, so as to provide extra accommodation for students and additional farm buildings for instructional purposes, The College has no endowment, no reserve funds and only one scholarship. This last is subscribed by former students and maintains one girl in training. It is hoped that the present Appeal may result in the raising of more than £20,000, in which case the surplus will be devoted to the more urgent of these needs, such as the creation of an Endowment Fund and the establishment of additional scholarships.

Former students of the College have already formed a Committee to raise funds, and have collected over £1,300. The sixty present students and staff made themselves responsible for £300, and have already this sum in hand.

Will you help by giving a donation now, or by promising to send one before October 1st, 1929, to the Hon. Treasurer, Midlands Appeal Committee, Mr. H. S. FELLOWS, Lloyds Bank, Colmore Row, Birmingham, or by organising a money-making effort, either now or during the coming autumn and winter. Donations and promises of help will be gratefully received in the Information Tent outside the courtyard.

4

Extract from Studley College 'Exhibition and Sale' brochure, 1929. The event was opened by HRH The Duchess of York (Queen Elizabeth The Queen Mother). Page 12 shows the Bell Brewery and Pub in readiness for the occasion. *Editor's collection.*

Above: The Orangery at Studley Castle, 1910, now long gone. *Editor's collection.*

Right: Learning to plough at Studley College. The main stable block can just be seen in the background. *Courtesy Kath Weaver (née Mills).*

Below: When Rover's heritage department moved in, all the outbuildings and stable blocks were used to store their collection of vehicles, meanwhile various unrestored vehicles were left dotted around outside, c.1988. *Editor's collection.*

Old Castle is a timber framed property built during the 16th century on the site of an 11th century castle. The building gradually fell into disrepair and is seen here in 1897 showing signs of dilapidation. Fortunately it was eventually renovated. *Courtesy SLHG.*

Old Castle today. The property is listed grade II*. *Courtesy Judy Ash.*

OLD CASTLE, STUDLEY,
CLOSE TO STUDLEY CHURCH.

TO BE SOLD BY AUCTION, BY

CHARLES WHITE,

On FRIDAY NEXT, OCTOBER 6, 1876,

Upon the Premises in the occupation of Mrs. Cook, the whole of the Household

FURNITURE,

Comprising—Seg-seated, Cane, Windsor, Arm, and Easy Chairs, two-leaf mahogany Dining, Pembroke, and other Tables, oak Bookcase with bureau combined, mahogany Chest Drawers, oval-front oak Corner Cupboard, Gentleman's oak Press, framed Pictures, antique China, three Feather Beds; Kitchen, Scullery, and Chamber Appendages, d ther Effects

Yard, Scullery, &c.

LOT
1 Twelve-gallon barrel
2 Dough steel
3 Small muslin kettle
4 Cucumber frame
5 Two small casks
6 Iron pot and fryingpan
7 Six brass candlesticks
8 Scales and weights
9 Stoneware
10 Water tub
11 Basket and two round tubs
12 Flight six steps
13 Saw-bench and two saws
14 Large copper pot
15 Two forks and spade
16 Steelyards, equal to 875 lbs.
17 Small ditto
18 Large cheese tub
19 Butter-tub and boards
20 Two cream tins
21 Two ditto
22 Kitchen, window, staircase, and hoops
23 Draught-plate and clothes line
24 Round table
25 Sundries

Entrance Hall

26 Six Windsor chairs
27 Three ditto
28 Old oil painting
29 Pair framed pictures
30 Umbrella stand
31 Hall table on iron stand
32 Hat stand
33 Door mat and iron scraper

Ante-Room

34 Oak book-case, with bureau combined, fitted with secret and small drawers
35 Oak table
36 Paper tray
37 Oak circular-front cupboard
38 Pair decanters and stands
39 Toast rack and glass dish

LOT
40 Six silver teaspoons
41 Pair silver sugar tongs
42 Various teaware
43 Metal teapot and various glassware
44 Sundry earthenware in lots
45 Eight custard glasses
46 Glass cake-stand
47 Five glass dishes
48 Two glass cups and sundry glass
49 Six-hole furnished cruet
50 Three-hole furnished liquor cruet
51 Pair decanters
52 Oak press on chest, very good
53 Oak round table
54 Plate warmer
55 Arm chair

Parlour

56 Mahogany sideboard, fitted with cellarette and drawers
57 Fancy two-leaf mahogany table
58 Mahogany dining table, with moveable leaf
59 Two-leaf mahogany table
60 Five various pictures
61 Six ditto
62 Oil painting, in gilt frame, "John Campbell in the character of Hamlet"
63 Easy chair, in morocco
64 Covered sofa
65 Six horse hair seated chairs
66 Two arm chairs to match
67 Fender and irons
68 Carpet to room
69 Fancy fire board
70 Chimney glass, in gilt frame
71 Small stand
72 Two stools
73 Pair curtains and cornice
74 Wheel barometer
75 Chimney ornaments
76 Hearth rug
77 Pair hassocks
78 Ink stand

Ancient China

79 Pair delf painted ancient scent vases

LOT
80 Ancient punch bowl
81 Two ancient basses
82 Six ditto cups, plate, and three saucers
83 Pair ancient glass vases, and fancy vase
84 Pair painted ancient vases
85 Sundry ornaments
86 Quantity books

Sitting Room

87 Arm Windsor chair
88 Arm ditto
89 Large chair
90 Two-leaf Pembroke table
91 One-leaf deal table
92 Round stand
93 Curtains and cornice
94 Butler's tray
95 Card table
96 Coal vase
97 Iron fender and irons
98 Ditto ditto
99 Oak cruet
100 Mahogany Pembroke table
101 Double barrel gun
102 Six dish covers
103 Knife box and knives
104 Table lamp
105 American timepiece
106 Fancy ditto

Chamber No. 1

107 Tent steads and dimity furniture, and straw mattress
108 Goose feather bed
109 Wool mattress
110 Coloured counterpane
111 Pair blankets
112 Chest drawers
113 Ditto
114 Ditto
115 Six rug chairs
116 Mahogany night commodes
117 Fancy work cushion
118 Curtains, and blinds to window
119 Carpet to room
120 Brass mounted fender

LOT
121 Nine pieces green-and-white chamber-ware
122 Slop pail, water can and foot pan
123 Three pictures
124 Napkin airer, and mat
125 Pair tables

Landing

126 Large arm chair
127 Flour tub
128 Bed pan
129 Door mat, carpets and rugs

Chamber No. 2

130 Four-post steads and furniture
131 Feather bed
132 Three mattresses
133 Wash stand
134 Mahogany chest five drawers
135 Fancy ancient timepiece
136 Mahogany stand
137 Toilet glass
138 Napkin airer
139 Four rug-seated chairs
140 Three ditto
141 Carpet to room
142 Chamber-ware
143 Brass mounted fender
144 Framed picture
145 Mahogany chest five drawers
146 Small chest four ditto
147 Toilet glass
148 Set three chimney ornaments
149 Tent steads and furniture
150 Set chintz furniture

Store Room

151 Set four-post steads
152 Half tester ditto
153 Six horse-hair seated chairs
154 Three seg seated chairs
155 Wash stand
156 Beach cornice
157 Quantity hanging paper

BUSINESS AT ONE O'CLOCK.

Catalogues may be had from Place of Sale, or from the Auctioneer, Redditch, Alcester, and Bromsgrove.

W. T. HEMING, MACHINE PRINTING OFFICE, REDDITCH.

1876 poster for the sale of all household items pertaining to Old Castle. *Courtesy SLHG.*

Above: Studley Fire Brigade, taken on the high street c.1940s. *Courtesy Brian Crow.*

Left: Studley Fire Brigade, Remembrance Sunday, 2008. *Courtesy Brian Crow.*

Below: Studley Fire Station, Bell Lane, during 2009. Sadly, due to budget cuts, the station was closed in 2013. *Courtesy Judy Ash.*

Alcester Road in 1907. In 1912 the wall to the left of the black and white cottage was demolished to make way for Manor Park Road (now Manor Road). To the far left is the original Conservative Club. *Courtesy SLHG.*

STUDLEY. 87.

Below: On the 17th May, 1968 a gas leak somewhere between Gunners Lane and Alcester Road led to a major explosion and a devastating fire. The original Conservative Club was demolished and a much plainer property was built in its place. Here Studley resident and fireman Geoff Vale can be seen operating the pump. *Courtesy Geoff Vale.*

Teenagers outside Studley Youth Centre, High Street, during the late 1980s. *Courtesy SLHG.*

1st Studley Scout Group heading down Castle Road during 1995. *Courtesy Karen Marshall.*

In November 1979, 480 Squadron Air Cadets opened a base at the top of the Foredraught, just off Pool Road. In 1981 the Squadron acquired a DH Vampire T11 aircraft (above). The aircraft was displayed outside until 1991 when the group moved to the other side of the carpark. At this time the plane was donated to Yorkshire Air Museum. *Courtesy John Shakles.*

1st Studley Scout Group proudly celebrating their Golden Anniversary year in 2010. In order to mark the occasion a gold edge was added to their scarlet neckers. *Courtesy Karen Marshall.*

The original Studley Village Hall, High Street, c.1980. Home to Studley's popular amateur dramatics organisation The Cygnet Players. *Editor's collection.*

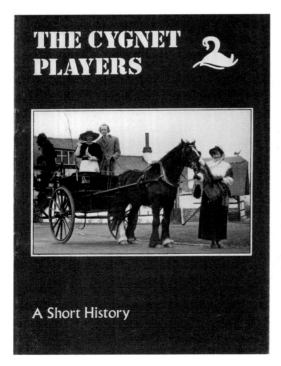

'The Cygnet Players: A Short History' covered the group's first 18 years. It was also the first book, Studley based, Brewin Books published forty years ago in 1976. *Editor's collection.*

The Cygnet Players' Sandwich board men advertising 'Toad of Toad Hall' on the corner of Alcester Road and Bell Lane, February 1975. *Editor's collection.*

The Cygnet Players' Tim Eagleton in 'And So To Bed' at Studley Village Hall, 1977.
Editor's collection.

STUDLEY OPERATIC SOCIETY
PRESENTS FOR ITS 80th ANNIVERSARY PRODUCTION

30p

The
GIPSY PRINCESS

(by arrangement with NODA LIMITED on
behalf of JOSEF WEINBERGER LTD.)

Music by ....*Emmerich Kalman*

Book by ....*Conrad Carter*

Lyrics by.............................*Phil Park*

Music Arranged by ....*Ronald Hanmer*

Musical Director ....*John Parker*

Assistant Producer/Choreographer ......*Maree Martin*

The Entire Production
under the Direction of...............*Denis Charlton*

MONDAY 7th APRIL TO SATURDAY 12th APRIL 1986
EVENINGS AT 7.30p.m.
SATURDAY MATINEE AT 2.30p.m.
AT THE LEYS HIGH SCHOOL THEATRE REDDITCH

AN AMATEUR PRODUCTION.

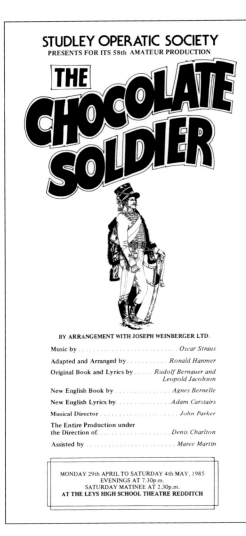

STUDLEY OPERATIC SOCIETY
PRESENTS FOR ITS 58th AMATEUR PRODUCTION

THE CHOCOLATE SOLDIER

BY ARRANGEMENT WITH JOSEPH WEINBERGER LTD.

Music by ....*Oscar Straus*

Adapted and Arranged by ....*Ronald Hanmer*

Original Book and Lyrics by .....*Rudolf Bernauer and
Leopold Jacobson*

New English Book by ....*Agnes Bernelle*

New English Lyrics by...............*Adam Carstairs*

Musical Director ....*John Parker*

The Entire Production under
the Direction of...................*Denis Charlton*

Assisted by ....*Maree Martin*

MONDAY 29th APRIL TO SATURDAY 4th MAY, 1985
EVENINGS AT 7.30p.m.
SATURDAY MATINEE AT 2.30p.m.
AT THE LEYS HIGH SCHOOL THEATRE REDDITCH

Above: Programme from Studley Operatic Society's 'The Gipsy Princess', 1986. Programme from Studley Operatic Society's 'The Chocolate Soldier', 1985. *Editor's collection.*

Left: Studley Operatic Society's performance of 'Rose Marie', 1984. The organisation was established in 1906 and still produces an annual performance. *Courtesy SLHG.*

Studley High School Amateur Dramatics Society (SHADS) Carnival Float taking part in the 1988 Studley Carnival procession, Alcester Road. *Courtesy Alan Brewin.*

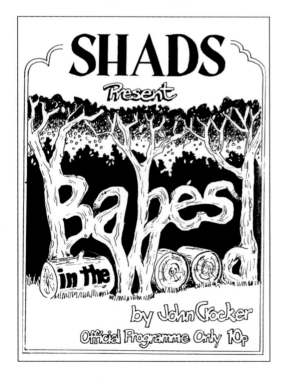 

Programme from SHADS' 'Babes in the Wood'. *Courtesy SLHG.*
Programme from SHADS' 'Robinson Crusoe'. *Courtesy SLHG.*

A lovely period shot of Holt Gardens based decorators Raymond Rawlins Ltd taken in the late 1960s. Pictured are Ray Rawlins, Seymour Sutor and George Woodward. *Courtesy Irene Deaner (née Sutor).*

Founded in 1942, Hunts of Studley originally specialised in transporting cattle. The business later expanded operating a fleet of vehicles providing cattle transportation, furniture removals and a parcel carrying service. The business was subsequently split with Hunts retaining the furniture removal side and the Allely family taking over the livestock transport. Today, based in Redditch and with seven locations, Hunts of Redditch still thrives. *Courtesy Adam Oakley.*

Studley based haulage firm Allelys was founded in 1959 by Maurice Allely and originally specialised in livestock movements. Pictured here are Maurice, Hector and Gwen Allely in the yard with the fleet as purchased from Arthur Hunt in 1959. *Courtesy David Allely.*

Above: A Dodge hay lorry parked on the Slough outside Benavon in the 1960s. *Courtesy David Allely.*

Left: Today the business is renowned for its heavy haulage operations. In 2013 this included transporting the biggest-ever load on Britain's roads, a giant transformer removed from Didcot power station.

Studley Garage together with the Barley Mow, c.1920s. *Courtesy Raymond Lamb.*

Graham C. Hill with Horace Ireland and R. Tandy in 1925. *Courtesy Raymond Lamb.*

Established in 1911 Studley Garage was originally based in the former brewery building attached to the Barley Mow. In 1923 Graham C. Hill purchased the business and quickly expanded it. During the 1930s land was purchased opposite on the Alcester Road and a much larger garage was built complete with ornate curved tower. After his death in 1972 his children ran the business until 1985 when it was sold and renamed Studley Self Serve. Sadly the garage became unprofitable and was sold to the Aldi Supermarket chain who demolished it in 2007.

Information courtesy Raymond Lamb.

A tractor parked outside the new premises of Studley Garage, Alcester Road. *Courtesy SLHG.*

An air force pilot in World War 1, Mr. G. C. Hill, who was responsible for the growth of the old-established Studley Garage, can look back on twenty-five years' service on Alcester R.D.C. of which he was once chairman. He considers that the most important development seen in Studley during the past half-century has been the establishment of Needle Industries Ltd. He doesn't think that Studley will improve greatly in the future, and fears – in common with other villagers – that it may be swallowed up by Redditch.

Article on Graham C. Hill, 1969.

Reverse view of the curved tower. *Courtesy SLHG.*

Above: During the 1950s Redditch Air Training Corps were given a Spitfire by the Air Ministry but could not find anywhere to store it. Graham C. Hill agreed for its assembly and storage behind the garage. With the agreement of Priory Farm's Eric Langston the plane was moved to the field next to the garage. Mr Hill later attempted to purchase the plane but, unfortunately, the Air Ministry ordered that it be broken up for scrap.
Information courtesy Roger Hill.
Pic courtesy Phillip Wainwright.

Left: Another view of the Spitfire, from Fleece Hill. *Courtesy Bob Pinfield.*

Above: Studley Self Serve in 1997.
Courtesy John Shakles.

Right: During the 1980s Studley
Garage was a main dealer for
Vauxhall-Opel and Bedford
vehicles. *Editor's collection.*

Below: The site has now become
an Aldi supermarket.
Editor's collection.

The Lea-Francis
"ACE OF SPADES"

The philosophy behind the design and production of the new Lea-Francis is exactly that of the founders of the original business in 1895.

Richard Lea and Graham Francis were determined to build cycles, motor cycles and cars to the highest possible standards of quality with regard to materials, workmanship and integrity of design.

Lea-Francis products were always attractive in appearance and possessed a high degree of individuality.

The new car continues the tradition and will provide ageless pleasure and satisfaction to owners who will enjoy, in addition, the exclusivity which limited production will provide - indeed it is unlikely that any two cars will be identical.

The care and attention with which each car is built results in the provision of something more than a means of transport from A to B. Indeed it would appear sacrilege to subject a Lea-Francis to the rough and tumble of everyday use, rather it is to be savoured for pleasure motoring and special occasions. It is more than a motor car, it is a jewel and an ambassador for British craftsmanship.

The Lea-Francis "Ace of Spades" is a two-seater sports saloon constructed from aluminium extruded sections and castings with hand beaten panels in 16 gauge aluminium.

Interior trimmed in Connolly hide, Wilton carpet and West of England cloth headlining. Fully adjustable seats, electrically operated windows, fixed rear quarter lights, and large trimmed rear parcel shelf. Fully trimmed boot with vertically mounted spare wheel, all trimmed in matching Wilton carpet. Veneered dashboard and door cappings, laminated glass all round, with concealed sun vizors and flush fitting door handles. With a choice of colour to customers order.

SPECIFICATION

Box section chassis 5" x 2" side members, bolt on front cross member 4" x 2" channel section cruciform

Aluminium coachwork throughout

Wheel Base 109" Track Front: 52⅞ Rear 53½

Torsion Bar I.F.S.

Leaf Spring Suspension

Conventional Hypoid Rear Axle 3.6 to 1

Jaguar 3½ Litre 2 OHC. 6 Cylinder Engine, 5 speed gearbox

Front Brakes by Disc - diameter: 11"

Rear Brakes by Drum - diameter: 9"

Vacuum Servo Operation

Lever Type Central Handbrake

Rack and Pinion Steering

Single Hardy-Spicer Propshaft

Radiator - Marston Ultra Fine Film

Twin Exhaust System with Double Silencers

Rudge 15" Wire Wheels with 205 x 15 Dunlop tyres

Petrol Tank capacity: 20 gallons

Stainless Steel Radiator Shell and Slats, and the majority of small fittings are also stainless

Sundym Glass in Windscreen

Smith Heater/de-mister installation

Pioneer Stereo Radio/Cassette Player

Connolly Hide

Wilton Carpet

Satinwood Veneers

Lea-Francis Cars Ltd.

Hardwick House, Castle Road, Studley, Warwickshire
B80 7AF. Tel: Studley (052785) 2377.

A.B. Price Limited

Specialists in the maintenance and repair of high grade cars for over 40 years. Comprehensive coachbuilding facilities available, notably specialists in the repair of aluminium panels, wood frames, trim, paintwork.

Separate division for complete rebuilds of classic and vintage cars. © Copyright Lea-Francis Cars Ltd.

Lea-Francis cars are subject to a continuous development programme and specifications may change from those detailed in this leaflet.

Above and below: In 1962 Barrie Price purchased the Lea-Francis car division name and assets. In 1980 from his base at Hardwick House in Castle Road, along with high end car repairs, he started hand producing a totally new model called 'Ace of Spades'. According to the Lea-Francis owners club only five were painstakingly built. The editor remembers seeing the car at the 1992 NEC Motor Show which is also where he picked up the brochure shown here. *Editor's collection.*

Above: Taft's Garage, Alcester Road c.1930s. The garage was later renamed Park Garage referring to the fields next to the garage known as Studley Park. After further expansion the name was once again changed to Newpark Garage. Today, it is the village's sole surviving petrol station. It is now known as DC Edginton and Sons. *Courtesy SLHG.*

Right: 1980s advert for Newpark Garage extolling the values of the new Austin Metro. The garage previously had a Renault franchise before switching to Austin Rover and later becoming independent. The editor remembers the petrol attendant filling his mother's car with National fuel and collecting the tokens to get a Corgi petrol tanker! *Editor's collection.*

AUSTIN ROVER

COME AND DRIVE BRITAIN'S BEST LITTLE CAR.

METRO

Before you choose a small family hatchback, check out the range that can get up to 64.1MPG,[1] go 12,000 miles between services[2] and is covered by a free 6-year corrosion warranty.

From the affordable City to the exhilarating MG Metro Turbo, you'll see why Britain's best selling little car is Britain's best little car at the best little price.

By a long way.

BRITISH CARS MEAN BRITISH JOBS.

NEWPARK GARAGE LTD

109 Alcester Road Studley B80 7NW   Telephone 2297 & 3940

[1] Official D.O.T. Figures. Metro 1.0HLE Urban Cycle 46.4MPG (6.1L per 100KM), Constant 56MPH 64.1MPG (4.4L per 100KM), Constant 75MPH 45.3MPG (6.2L per 100KM). [2] Or one full year, whichever comes first (excepting automatic and turbocharged models).

Above: Looking down New Road onto the Alcester Road c.1957. Lloyds Bank's original premises. *Courtesy Phillip Wainwright.*

Right: Lloyds' premises turned into Bonkeys Motor Cycles. The building is currently home to Synergy Hair and Beauty. *Courtesy Simon Mee.*

Below: c.1957 before relocating to Haydon House Midland Bank were based further down the Alcester Road at what is now Chiropractic (UK). *Courtesy Phillip Wainwright.*

STUDLEY 2089

Above: After the demise of Needle Industries the Co-operative purchased the old Central Works site and built one of Studley's most controversial buildings, Leo's, seen here in the early 1990s. *Courtesy SLHG.*

Left: Still under Co-operative control, Leo's was later rebranded Pioneer and repainted yellow and green. The photo shows the rear entrance in Marble Alley taken during the 1990s. *Courtesy John Shakles.*

TR Allen's shop, Alcester Road, 1887 plus shed with thatched roof. *Courtesy Bill McCarthy.*

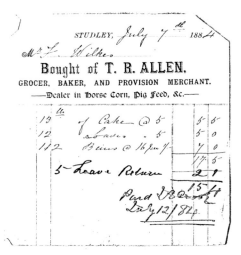

Above: A receipt from TR Allen for cakes, loaves and buns, dated 1884. *Courtesy Bill McCarthy.*

Left: TR Allen butchers (left) and stores (right) c.1980. The stores became Roy's Bikes before falling derelict. *Courtesy John Shakles.*

Luggage Label, Midland Railway, Studley and Astwood Bank.

Midland Railway. P. F. 70.

STUDLEY and ASTWOOD BANK

Staff look on at Studley and Astwood Bank Station, Green Lane, c.1920. *Editor's collection.*

Although the line was axed by Dr Beeching the Station house still remains and is now residential accommodation. The station closed fully in 1964 and, judging by the neglect, this shot looks to have been taken close to that date. *Courtesy SLHG.*

Above: The Nativity of the Blessed Virgin Mary, otherwise known at St. Mary's Church, Castle Road, 2008. Built in the early 12th century the Church is listed grade II*. *Editor's collection.*

Above: In 2012 it received a new porch to mark the 900th anniversary of the Church. *Courtesy John C Groom.*

Left: A much earlier photo taken c.1930. *Editor's collection.*

A 1920s shot of St Mary's Roman Catholic Church, Alcester Road. The building was opened in 1853 and was designed by Charles Hansom, the brother of Joseph Hansom who was responsible for the design of Birmingham Town Hall and the Hansom cab. It is currently listed grade II. *Editor's collection.*

Bottom left: Studley Baptist Church, New Road, 2006. Studley Baptist church was formed in 1847, the following year in 1848 this Chapel was built. *Courtesy John Shakles.*

Bottom right: Studley Methodist Church, Alcester Road, 2016. Studley's first Methodist Chapel originally sat on the site now occupied by Studley Conservative Club. The foundation stone for this second Chapel was laid on 20th May 1872 with the building opening a year later. In 2016 the property benefitted from a £250,000 revamp. *Courtesy Gwynn Bamford.*

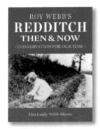
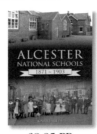

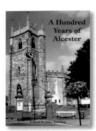
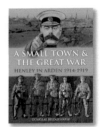
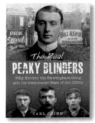

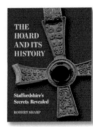

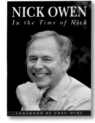
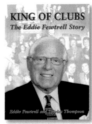
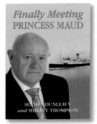
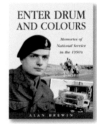